Candy!

Candy!

A Sweet Selection of Fun and Easy Recipes

Laura Dover Doran

Lark Books

Asheville, North Carolina

Art Direction and Production: Celia Naranjo
Photography: Evan Bracken
Editorial Assistance: Evans Carter
Proofreader: Val Anderson

Library of Congress Cataloging-in-Publication Data
Doran, Laura Dover, 1970-
    Candy! : a sweet selection of fun and easy recipes / by Laura Dover Doran. —1st ed.
    p. cm.
    Includes index.
    ISBN 1-57990-055-0 (hardcover) ISBN 1-57990-111-5 (paperback)
    1. Candy. I. Title.
TX791.D67 1998
641.8'53—dc21   98-9654
                                                                   CIP

10 9 8 7 6 5 4 3 2 1

First Edition

Published by Lark Books
50 College St.
Asheville, NC 28801, US

Distributed by Random House, Inc., in the United States, Canada,
the United Kingdom, Europe, and Asia
Distributed in Australia by Capricorn Link (Australia) Pty Ltd., P.O. Box 6651, Baulkham
Hills Business Centre, NSW 2153, Australia
Distributed in New Zealand by Tandem Press Ltd., 2 Rugby Rd.,
Birkenhead, Auckland, New Zealand

Printed in Hong Kong by Oceanic Graphic Printing Productions Ltd.

ISBN 1-57990-055-0 (hardcover)   ISBN 1-57990-111-5 (paperback)

For my grandmother, Georgia Shuford,
whose work in the kitchen made my childhood sweeter

Acknowledgments

First, I would like to thank Scott Gerken, who prepared the candy for photography, except for the candy on pages 34, 38, 48, 56, 82, and 122 (prepared by the author), the fudge on page 88 (prepared by Sandra Dover), the seafoam on page 102 (prepared by Georgia Shuford), the popcorn balls on page 114 (prepared by Will Albrecht, Wes Albrecht, and Dawn Cusick), and the unsugared hard candy on page 28 (prepared by Rob Pulleyn).

Special thanks to the following for contributing and testing recipes: Wes Albrecht, Will Albrecht, Val Anderson, Brian and Robin Caskey, Dawn Cusick, Patrick Doran, Sandra Dover, Susie Gray, Donna Hudson, Dana Irwin, Celia Naranjo, Rob Pulleyn, Deanne Shuford, Georgia Shuford, Elaine Thompson, Nicole Tuggle, Phyllis Utley, Gladys Wilson, and the staff of Lark Books.

I would also like to extend gratitude to Bob Carter at Bakers C. & C. (Salt Lake City, Utah) for supplying candy molds, as well as to the folks at Loran Oils (Lansing, Michigan) and Hershey Foods Corporation (Hershey, Pennsylvania) for providing useful information. And many thanks to Art Director Celia Naranjo, for her careful attention to photography and design.

Contents

Introduction

I spent hour upon hour as a young girl sitting on a stool by the countertop in my grandmother's kitchen watching her work. While my friends and sisters were outside on bikes or glued to the TV, I was in the kitchen with Gran. She would hum or chat with me or maybe stare out the window as she stirred and mixed and kneaded something delicious—often something sweet. When I visit Gran now, I am still drawn to her kitchen, because it symbolizes all that is wonderful about cooking. The excitement of knowing a happy occasion is at hand and food is to be prepared—whether it's a holiday meal or just Sunday lunch—is irreplaceable.

It has been my experience that candy evokes positive associations in just about everyone, because it is great fun both to give and receive. I have found that, although many people enjoy candy immensely, most are reluctant to try making it. Indeed, the misconception that candymaking requires serious equipment and years of training is prevalent.

Candymaking is actually quite simple and often requires only a few ingredients and very basic knowledge. It has been my intention to present candymaking in a simple and straightforward manner in this book. The equipment and ingredients you will need, as well as basic candymaking information, are discussed in detail, and the recipes are presented in easy, step-by-step format, with color photographs of each recipe.

Good luck and happy candymaking!

Candymaking Ingredients

CHOCOLATE

It is very important to use high-quality chocolate. The best way to determine the quality of chocolate is to taste it. Chocolate that tastes good straight from the container will taste the same in the recipe. Do not use unsweetened chocolate for candymaking.

Bittersweet or *semisweet chocolates*, also referred to as *dark chocolates*, are chocolates in which cocoa butter is added back to the cocoa liquor, as well as lecithin (an emulsifier to keep the cocoa butter from separating), vanilla, and sugar. Bittersweet has less sugar and usually more chocolate liquor added than semisweet; bittersweet and semisweet are interchangeable in recipes. (Europeans tend to use more bittersweet chocolate and Americans more semisweet.)

Higher-quality chocolates, sometimes called *coverture chocolate* or *dipping chocolate*, are usually sold in large blocks and have a higher cocoa butter content. They are also sometimes available in flat, button-shaped pieces, which look remarkably like compound coating (see below); be sure you are buying what you intend to buy. Since they have a higher percentage of cocoa butter, coverture chocolates must be tempered (see page 11).

Milk chocolate has a milder flavor and is the most widely available form of chocolate; it is a combination of dry milk solids, sugar, lecithin, cocoa butter, and flavorings. If a recipe calls for *milk* or *white chocolate*, do not substitute. White chocolate, sometimes called *confectioners' coating*, is not actually chocolate, as it contains no cocoa liquor. A common mistake is to confuse white chocolate, which is cocoa-butter based, with *compound coating* (also called *summer coating*), which is vegetable-fat based. Compound coating does not need to be tempered and can be used for dipping. Though compound coating has a different flavor than real chocolate and does not produce the highest quality candy, it is less expensive and is not affected by excess heat, as is dipping chocolate. It is also great to use when practicing your dipping technique.

Store chocolate—wrapped in aluminum foil, not plastic wrap—at room temperature in a moisture-free environment, not in the refrigerator. Milk and white chocolate can be stored up to a year and dark chocolates indefinitely.

Melting Chocolate

Chop chocolate into very small pieces for melting, and always melt it slowly over hot, but never boiling, water in a double boiler. Do not allow any water (or any other liquid) to drop into the chocolate. A very small drop of water will cause the chocolate to gum up. Stir the chocolate often as it melts. More commonly, people are using microwave ovens to melt chocolate. If you choose this method, you need to set the microwave for very short intervals of time (no more than 20 or 25 seconds) and stir between each.

Tempering Chocolate

When using chocolate that contains cocoa butter for dipping or molding, the chocolate must be *tempered*. This simply means it is melted, cooled somewhat, then brought back to the dipping temperature. Otherwise, the chocolate will take a very long time to set up and will have gray streaks (called *bloom*) in it when it does set up. (Bloom can also be caused by excessive humidity and does not affect the flavor, only the appearance, of the candy.) Tempered chocolate is shiny, flavorful, and goes on in a thin layer.

In general, chocolate chips or blocks of chocolate available in most supermarkets do not need to be tempered, though they can be tempered to achieve a shinier surface with dipping and coating. Higher quality chocolate sold in specialty shops, gourmet food stores, and through mail order will need to be tempered. NOTE: If tempered chocolate cools completely, it will need to be retempered.

Here is the quickest and easiest, though not the only, method for tempering chocolate. Bring water to a boil in the bottom of a double boiler. Chop 1 pound (454 g) of chocolate into small bits, divide into thirds, and set one-third aside. Put the other two-thirds of the chocolate in the double boiler over the hot (not simmering, as with regular chocolate melting) water and melt. Clip a thermometer to the side of the pan; do not let the chocolate get over 120° F (84° C). Stir the chocolate frequently with a rubber spatula until it is melted. When the chocolate is melted, remove double boiler from heat. Lift the top of the double boiler off the water and wipe the bottom of the pot dry. Stir in the remaining chocolate pieces, a quarter of the remaining portion at a time, melting completely between each addition. When all the chocolate is melted, you will have tempered chocolate.

BUTTER

I always use butter, never margarine. Many people insist on using margarine, but the flavor is definitely different and the results are never as good. (And whether it is healthier is very questionable.) Having said that, you can substitute margarine for butter in most candy recipes, with the exception of toffee recipes. Use butter when it is the predominant flavor, and, if you must, margarine when another flavor is the focus of the recipe. Always use unsalted butter in candy recipes. It has a fresher taste and you will be able to control the salt content of your candy. Unsalted butter spoils more easily than salted butter, so be sure to keep it refrigerated or frozen for longer storage times.

MILK PRODUCTS

You can use skim, low-fat, or whole milk in candymaking, though keep in mind that candy made with milk with a lower fat content will not be as rich. If you desire richer candy, you can substitute *whipping cream* (also called *heavy cream*)—whipping cream will not stick to the saucepan as readily as milk and, thus, will require less stirring. Also, using whipping cream decreases the likelihood of your candy becoming granular.

Whipping cream has a butterfat content between 35% and 40%. *Heavy whipping cream* has an even higher butterfat content. Do not substitute evaporated milk for whipping cream. *Sweetened condensed milk* is whole milk with added sugar and less water. Do not substitute sweetened condensed milk for regular milk in candy recipes.

LIQUEURS

Liqueurs, or alcohol or brandy with added sugar and flavoring, are often used in candymaking. Be aware that less is more with liqueur; use high-quality liqueur and be careful not to add too much. Liqueurs commonly used in candymaking are cognac, port, dark rum, Irish cream, Grand Marnier, Kahlúa (coffee), amaretto (almond), Chambord (black raspberry), Cointreau, curaçao (orange-flavored), kirschwasser (cherry), framboise (raspberry), Frangelico (hazelnut), and Nocello (walnut). Usually an "airplane bottle" is enough for candy recipes, so check the recipe before you invest in a full bottle. Store liqueurs sealed in a cool, dry spot.

SUGAR

Sugar is probably the ingredient most associated with candy—it sweetens, of course, but also sometimes enhances other flavors. *Granulated sugar*, or white table sugar, is the most commonly used type, but when a finer texture is required, *confectioners' sugar* (also called *powdered sugar*) is sometimes called for. Confectioners' sugar is simply finely ground granulated sugar mixed with cornstarch to prevent caking. (In Canada, confectioners' sugar is called *icing sugar*.)

Somewhere in between granulated sugar and confectioners' sugar is *superfine sugar* (also called *bar sugar* or *caster sugar*), which is more highly granulated than regular granulated sugar. To make your own superfine sugar, grind granulated sugar in a blender or a food processor for about one minute.

Brown sugar is less refined than granulated sugar. It contains a small amount of molasses and is extremely rich in flavor. Whether to use light or dark brown sugar is strictly a matter of personal preference, although light brown sugar is generally preferred in candymaking. Always pack brown sugar into the measuring cup and level with a table knife.

Store all sugar at room temperature in an airtight container.

LIQUID SUGARS

Corn syrup is refined from cornstarch with water added, and serves to reduce the graininess and prevent sugar crystallization in candy recipes. Light and dark corn syrup are interchangeable, though dark syrup contains molasses, is less refined, and has a stronger (and different) flavor. Be careful not to use too much corn syrup, as it causes candy to take longer to set up and will make hard candies more sticky.

Molasses has a very distinctive flavor—and is quite delicious in a number of candy recipes. Use it only when called for, as the flavor is rich and sometimes too overpowering for some recipes.

Honey, the original sweetener, attracts moisture and, thus, softens candy. The flavor of honey varies considerably and depends on a number of factors, such as the type of flower the honey bees have fed upon.

NUTS

They add delicious flavor and texture to many a candy recipe and, although they are quite expensive, they are well worth the money. It is essential that all nuts be fresh. Because of their high fat content, nuts can become rancid. Nuts can be stored in the refrigerator or the freezer. Stored in the freezer, nuts will last up to a year. Some nuts that are great in candy are peanuts, pecans, almonds, macadamia nuts, pistachios, hazelnuts (filberts), pine nuts, and cashews.

Toasting Nuts

The flavor of many types of nuts is enhanced by roasting or toasting. Spread nuts out on a cookie sheet in an even layer and place cookie sheet in a preheated 325° F (160° C) oven for about 10 minutes, stirring once. Taste nuts, then place them back in the oven if necessary for as long as it takes to achieve the desired flavor. (Thinly sliced nuts will require a shorter toasting time.)

Candymaking Equipment

Candy Thermometer

An accurate thermometer is extremely helpful in candy-making, though it is possible to avoid recipes that require one. They are quite inexpensive, but don't get the cheapest one you can find, as it will probably not last very long. You will need one that reads in a range of 100° to 400° F (38° to 200° C) and that has 2-degree markings (5-degree markings are not accurate enough). It should read 212° F (100° C) at boiling point. Test your thermometer as often as you can by placing it in boiling water. If it reads higher than 212° F (100° C) after three or four minutes of boiling, then add the number of degrees that it is over to the temperature in the recipe. If it is lower, subtract from the recipe.

Make sure you always read the thermometer at eye level. A meat thermometer will not work in candy-making. Thermometers for use specifically with chocolate are available and are quite useful for this purpose. They register at 1-degree intervals and are extremely accurate.

Sometimes you will find candy recipes that tell you to cook syrup to a *soft-ball*, *firm-ball*, *hard-ball*, *soft-crack*, or *hard-crack stage*. This indicates how a small portion of syrup reacts when dropped in cold water and formed into a ball. To perform this test, place a small amount of syrup in a cup of very cold water.

Soft-ball stage (234° to 240° F or 110° to 115° C) is when the syrup makes a soft ball that flattens out when removed from the water.

Firm-ball stage (242° to 248° F or 115° to 120° C) is when the syrup makes a firm ball that does not flatten when it is removed from the water.

Hard-ball stage (250° to 268° F or 120° to 130° C) is when the syrup forms a hard, but still pliable ball when removed from the water.

░ Soft-crack stage (270° to 290° F or 130° to 145° C) is when the syrup separates into threads that are hard, but not brittle.

░ Hard-crack stage (300° to 310° F or 150° to 155° C) is when the syrup separates into threads that are hard and brittle.

Regardless of how confident you feel about how long your recipe should cook, it is always best to use a thermometer. Inaccurate temperature readings are among the most common candymaking goofs.

Saucepans

You can use a variety of pans for candymaking. You will sometimes need saucepans with lids, since using a lid in the first few minutes of cooking syrup will prevent your having to wash down the sides of the pan to prevent sugar crystallization. However, never use a lid with milk or heavy cream mixtures, as they have a tendency to cook up high and boil over. Use a large pan when cooking these candies.

Saucepans usually come in 1-quart (small), 2-quart (medium), and 3- or 4-quart (large) sizes, or close approximations thereof. Heavier-weight saucepans keep candy from scorching, so use these with cream-based or chocolate-based candies. Enamel cast-iron pans are superb for this purpose. Copper pans are great for cooking sugar-based mixtures, as copper conducts heat evenly and consistently.

A double-boiler setup is essential for melting chocolate. A glass setup is especially handy, as it allows you to visually monitor the bottom pan as well as the top one. You can improvise with a pan and a bowl, but make sure the bowl fits snugly into the pan and that water does not get into the bowl.

Marble Slab

Though it is certainly possible to make candy without a marble slab, it makes some recipes infinitely easier. Marble stays cold, which allows some candies to cool quickly. Before you invest in a marble slab, determine which types of candy you will make most often. Marble is especially useful in making pulled candies (page 112) and brittles, but a chilled jellyroll pan also works very well.

Dipping Tools

Dipping forks or candy dippers are useful for holding candies when dipping them in chocolate or compound coating. They are available at candy supply stores. Make your own candy dippers by breaking out the middle tines of a plastic fork or use a knife, toothpick, or any other tool that works.

Rubber Spatula, Metal Spatula, and Knives

You will find uses for all of these tools, especially for scraping candy mixtures from pans and mixing bowls. Rubber spatulas work well for stirring chocolate, because they do not absorb flavors. Metal scrapers aid in removing candy from cooling surfaces. You will need a sharp knife for cutting some candy, especially candy squares and caramels.

Pastry Brush

Use a pastry brush to wash down the sides of the pan when cooking sugar-based mixtures. This prevents crystallization on the sides of the pan. (This can also be accomplished by covering the mixture with a lid.) Wash pastry brushes in warm, soapy water, rinse thoroughly, squeeze out excess water, then allow to air dry. (You may wash in the dishwasher occasionally.)

Culinary Scissors

Particularly when making taffy (see page 112) and butter mints, it is sometimes necessary to cut candy strips into pieces with greased culinary scissors. Any pair of kitchen scissors will work fine for this purpose.

Electric Beater or Mixer

Either a portable or a stand-up mixer is a wonderful tool for candymaking. As candy thickens, it can become quite difficult to stir by hand. Usually, it is possible to do it by hand, but this method makes candymaking more tiresome than it needs to be. I strongly suggest investing in an electric rotary beater, at the very least.

Cookie Sheet/Baking Pan

When lined with wax paper or buttered, cookie sheets are perfect bases for chocolates and candies. Baking pans have a lip around the outer edge and are preferred when this is important—when making fudge, for example.

Molds

There is an amazing variety of candymaking molds out there. Metal or treated plastic are widely available. They are great for lollipops (see page 30) or hard candies. Plastic molds are ideal for molded chocolates (see page 92) and candies made with compound coatings, because they are flexible and make releasing candy easier.

BASIC CANDYMAKING TIPS

It is important that you read through the entire recipe once, then gather the necessary equipment and ingredients before you begin. Nothing is more frustrating than deciding to make a candy recipe and discovering—halfway through the process—that you have no whipping cream.

Measure all ingredients and place them within reach before you begin.

Give yourself enough time. Candymaking often requires slow cooking, constant stirring, and your undivided attention. If you are rushed, postpone the project until another day.

The weather makes a difference in candymaking. A perfect day for making candy is a clear, cool one. This is especially true of candies with a sugar syrup base.

For best results, begin with butter that is at room temperature.

High-quality ingredients are essential for high-quality candies. Don't skimp on ingredients.

Food color and flavoring should be the last—or among the last—ingredients to be added, because excess heat may alter colors or flavors unpredictably.

If at all possible, clean up immediately after making candy. Hardened sugar syrups or chocolate can be unbelievably difficult to remove from pans and other surfaces. If immediate attention is not possible, reheat hardened candy residue in pots over medium heat for easier cleanup. Use hot water and mild soap to clean countertops, stove tops, and utensils.

Keep at it. Your first dipped truffle will not be perfect, but you will improve with practice. And even if they don't look as wonderful as you had hoped, of course the flavor will still be as good.

Brittle, Bark, and Hard Candies

Candy Bows

I usually make these simple, sugary candies when I need a quick addition to a dessert table for a rather formal event. They also make adorable bow-ties for holiday gingerbread men.

Ingredients

½ cup (1 stick or 115 g) unsalted butter
1 cup (125 g) all-purpose flour
½ cup (170 g) light corn syrup
⅔ cup (80 g) brown sugar

Equipment

Large baking pan
Medium saucepan
Wooden spoon

Instructions

1. Butter a baking pan and set aside.

2. Melt the butter in the medium saucepan, then gradually stir in flour with a wooden spoon.

3. Add corn syrup and brown sugar. Bring mixture to a boil over high heat, then reduce heat to medium and continue to boil, stirring constantly.

4. After about seven minutes, pour the mixture into the buttered baking pan.

5. When the candy is comfortable to handle—which should take a minute or two—cut the sheet of candy into squares. Working quickly while the candy is still warm, pinch squares into bows. When the candy is completely cool, serve or store in an airtight container.

Yield: About 25 bows

Buttery Pistachio Brittle

The flavor and color of pistachios and the richness of butter make this brittle an interesting variation on traditional peanut brittle. Try macadamia nuts in place of pistachios for an extra-crunchy version.

Ingredients

2 tablespoons unsalted butter
½ cup (120 ml) water
1 cup (200 g) sugar
¼ cup (85 g) light corn syrup
Dash of salt
1 cup (150 g) shelled, chopped pistachio nuts
½ teaspoon baking soda
1 teaspoon vanilla extract

Equipment

Cookie sheet
Rubber spatula
Medium saucepan
Candy thermometer
Pastry brush
Wooden spoon
Small mixing bowl

26

Instructions

1. Before you begin, grease a cookie sheet and a spatula with butter.

2. In a medium saucepan, combine the butter, water, sugar, and corn syrup, and cook over high heat about 15 minutes or until the mixture registers 310° F (154° C) on a candy thermometer. To prevent the sugar from crystallizing, wash down the pan several times with a pastry brush that has been dipped in water.

3. Once the mixture reaches the desired temperature, quickly stir in the pistachio nuts and the salt with a wooden spoon. Make sure the nuts are coated completely.

4. In a small bowl (off the heat), combine the baking soda and the vanilla. Add the mixture to the brittle over the heat and stir.

5. Now that your brittle is completely cooked, you will need to work quickly before it begins to set up. Pour the brittle out onto the prepared cookie sheet and quickly spread it out with a wooden spoon. Set the brittle aside to cool.

6. After five minutes, run the buttered spatula under the brittle to loosen it from the cookie sheet. Set brittle aside. When the brittle has cooled completely, break it into pieces. Either serve at room temperature or store in an airtight container between pieces of wax paper. It will keep approximately one week.

Yield: About 45 pieces

Rock Candy

Rock candy, or traditional hard candy, is nothing more than the delicious union of sugar and water. The trick is heating the mixture to the correct temperature, which is easy to accomplish with a candy thermometer.

Ingredients

1¾ cups (350 g) sugar
½ cup (120 ml) water
½ cup (170 g) light corn syrup
Dash of salt
1 teaspoon flavoring of your choice
Confectioners' sugar for dusting

Equipment

Baking pan, 7 x 10 inches (18 x 25.5 cm)
Small, lidded saucepan
Pastry brush
Candy thermometer
Scissors

Instructions

1. Butter the baking pan and set aside.

2. In a small saucepan, combine the sugar, water, corn syrup, and a dash of salt, and stir mixture until the sugar dissolves. You may need to wash down the sides of the pan with a pastry brush that has been dipped in water, to prevent sugar crystallization.

3. Cover the pan and bring the mixture to a rolling boil. Remove the lid, place a thermometer in the pan, and cook the mixture to 250° F (120° C).

4. Add the flavoring and continue to cook for two to three minutes.

5. Pour into the prepared baking pan.

6. Cut the candy into strips with oiled scissors as soon as it is cool enough to handle, then cut the strips into squares, diamonds, or break into free-form shapes. When the candy has completely cooled, dust with confectioners' sugar.

    Yield: About 1 pound (454 g) of candy

Lollipops

For me, colorful candy lollipops will forever conjure wonderful childhood memories. Take your kids to the candy supply store, let them choose from the adorable lollipop molds that are now widely available, and make this recipe a family project.

Ingredients

1 cup (200 g) sugar
¼ cup (85 g) light corn syrup
¼ cup (60 ml) water
½ teaspoon salt
2 or 3 drops food coloring
Flavoring of your choice

Equipment

Lollipop molds or cookie sheet
Medium saucepan
Wooden spoon
Pastry brush
Candy thermometer
Sucker sticks

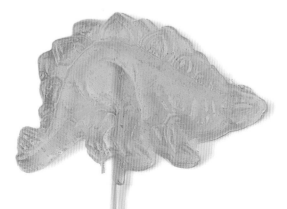

Instructions

1. If you are using lollipop molds, wash, dry, and butter the insides of the molds. If you do not have molds, butter a cookie sheet.

2. Combine the sugar, corn syrup, water, and salt in a saucepan and cook over medium-high heat, stirring with a wooden spoon until the mixture comes to a boil. Wash down the sides of the pan with a wet pastry brush, to prevent sugar crystallization.

3. When the mixture begins to boil, clip on a candy thermometer. Continue to boil until the mixture reaches 300° F (150° C). (Be patient.) Remove mixture from heat and blend in the food coloring and flavoring.

4. Immediately pour mixture into lollipop molds and press sucker sticks into the indentations in the molds. If you are using a cookie sheet, pour free-form circles on the sheet and place a sucker stick on each circle. Set aside to cool at room temperature. Store individually wrapped at room temperature.

Yield: 8 to 10 lollipops, depending on the mold size

Marbled Peanut Bark

Marbled bark is easy and makes an interesting addition to a candy tray. A few drops each of yellow and red food color (to make orange) added to the candy coating creates a wonderful black-and-orange Halloween treat.

Ingredients

8 ounces (226 g) vanilla-flavored candy coating, chopped
12 ounces (340 g) semisweet chocolate chips
1½ cups (165 g) peanuts

Equipment

Cookie sheet
Wax paper
Small saucepan
Double-boiler setup
Rubber spatula
Knife

Instructions

1. Line a cookie sheet with wax paper and set aside.

2. In a small saucepan, melt the vanilla-flavored coating over low heat. Make sure you stir constantly as the coating melts. Set aside.

3. In a double-boiler setup, melt the semisweet chocolate chips, again over low heat, stirring constantly with a rubber spatula.

4. When chocolate is melted, stir in peanuts.

5. Pour chocolate/peanut mixture onto the lined cookie sheet and use a spatula to spread. Gently pour vanilla coating mixture over the top of the chocolate, and use a knife to swirl the coating mixture.

6. Place in refrigerator until set, about one hour. Break bark into pieces and store in an airtight container.

Yield: About 30 pieces

English Toffee

A mouth-watering, buttery flavor and the crunch of toasted almonds make this traditional toffee recipe an instant crowd-pleaser. That is, if you are willing to share.

Ingredients

½ pound or 2 sticks (230 g) unsalted butter
1¼ cups (250 g) granulated sugar
1 tablespoon light corn syrup
¼ teaspoon salt
1 cup (85 g) roughly chopped toasted almonds

Equipment

Cookie sheet
Medium saucepan
Wooden spoon
Rubber spatula (optional)

Instructions

1. Butter a cookie sheet and set aside.

2. In a medium saucepan, combine the butter (at room temperature), sugar, corn syrup, and salt. Cook over medium-high heat and bring to a boil, stirring constantly with a wooden spoon, for about four minutes.

3. Turn the heat to high, add the almonds and cook, still stirring, for about seven minutes or until a light brown color is achieved.

4. Pour the mixture into the prepared cookie sheet, and spread it out evenly in the pan with a wooden spoon or a spatula. Set aside and allow toffee to cool.

5. When it is cool to the touch and hard, break the toffee into pieces and serve at room temperature. Store in an airtight container for up to 10 days.

Yield: About 60 pieces

Dana's Old-Fashioned Butterscotch

I adore this traditional butterscotch recipe, because it doesn't skimp on the molasses, giving the candy a deliciously tangy flavor. Place these in a pretty bowl by your entryway, and your guests may never leave!

Ingredients

2¾ cups (390 g) brown sugar
½ cup (115 g) butter
½ cup (170 g) molasses
2 tablespoons vinegar
2 tablespoons water
Dash of salt

Equipment

Cookie sheet
Wax paper
Large, heavy saucepan
Pastry brush
Candy thermometer

Instructions

1. Cover a cookie sheet with wax paper and set aside.

2. In a large saucepan, combine all the ingredients (brown sugar, butter, molasses, vinegar, water, and salt) and cook over high heat until sugar is dissolved. Wash down the sides of the saucepan with a pastry brush that has been dipped in cold water, to prevent sugar crystallization.

3. Clip a candy thermometer to the side of the pan and boil the mixture quickly until 300° F (150° C) is achieved.

4. Drop butterscotch from a spoon onto the waxed paper. Set aside and allow to harden.

Yield: About 40 pieces

Fruit Candies and Nut Confections

Lemon Gumdrops

These fruity little treats are a fun project to do with children, as they require a fair amount of contact with extremely sticky material. A great stress-relieving recipe!

Ingredients

2 cups (400 g) granulated sugar
½ cup (120 ml) water
1 box (four packets) plain gelatin and
½ cup (120 ml) water for dissolving gelatin
Juice of 1 lemon
Zest of 1 orange
2 to 4 drops yellow food coloring
½ cup (100 g) superfine sugar for rolling gumdrops

Equipment

Baking pan, 8 x 8 inches (20.5 x 20.5 cm)
Medium saucepan
Pastry brush
Small mixing bowl
Knife
Culinary scissors

Instructions

1. Butter the baking pan and set aside. (One of the keys to a successful batch of gumdrops is a well-buttered baking pan.)

2. Combine the sugar and ½ cup (120 ml) water in a medium saucepan and bring to a boil over medium heat. Stir constantly and wash down the sides of the pan with a pastry brush that has been dipped in cold water several times, to prevent sugar crystallization.

3. In a small mixing bowl, dissolve the gelatin in ½ cup (120 ml) water for five minutes. Add dissolved gelatin to the sugar mixture and continue to boil for 15 minutes, stirring constantly.

4. Add the lemon juice and orange zest to the syrup and boil for five more minutes. Add food coloring. Pour the mixture into the buttered baking dish and set aside to set up for about three hours.

5. After three hours, butter a knife, your fingers, and culinary scissors thoroughly. Cut the gummy substance into pieces (with the knife and/or scissors), roll into balls, and roll balls in superfine sugar. The balls will flatten out somewhat as they settle. Stored in an airtight container, these drops last for weeks.

Yield: About 70 gumdrops

Red Raspberry Jellies

Simple jelly squares can be flavored with any variety of fruit jam; raspberry is my favorite. These are delightful served with hot chocolate or chocolate candies.

Ingredients

¾ cup (150 g) sugar
1 cup (288 g) raspberry jam
½ cup (120 ml) water
2 (¼-ounce or 7-g) envelopes unflavored gelatin
¼ teaspoon citric acid
3 to 5 drops red food coloring
Confectioners' sugar (for dusting wax paper)
¾ cup (90 g) confectioners' sugar for rolling jellies

Equipment

Baking pan, 8 x 8 inches (20.5 x 20.5 cm)
Medium saucepan
Wooden spoon
Wax paper
Metal spatula or knife
Plastic wrap

Instructions

1. Butter the baking pan thoroughly and set aside.

2. Combine sugar, jam, water, gelatin, and citric acid in a medium saucepan over medium heat. (If you are using liquid pectin in granular form, first dissolve in 1 tablespoon of hot water.) Stir constantly with a wooden spoon. Boil the mixture for two minutes, stirring constantly. Stir in food coloring.

3. Pour mixture into prepared pan and place in the refrigerator for at least three hours.

4. When the jelly is firm, remove it from the refrigerator. Lightly sprinkle a piece of wax paper with confectioners' sugar. Use a metal spatula or a knife to loosen jelly from the edges of the pan and gently flip onto the wax paper.

5. Cut jelly into 1-inch (2.5-cm) squares. Roll each square in confectioners' sugar. Wrap each piece in plastic and store in an airtight container in the refrigerator.

Yield: About 64 pieces

Sugarplums

The word *plum* has conventionally been used to refer to any dried fruit—so don't be perplexed that there are no real plums in this recipe. One whiff of these deliciously spiced candies will instantly put you in the holiday spirit.

Ingredients

¼ cup (100 g) honey
1 teaspoon ground cinnamon
1 teaspoon ground allspice
½ teaspoon ground nutmeg
2 teaspoons orange zest
2 cups (170 g) finely chopped, toasted almonds
1 cup (170 g) finely chopped dried apricots
1 cup (198 g) finely chopped dates
⅛ cup (25 g) superfine sugar for rolling

Equipment

Medium mixing bowl
Wooden spoon

Instructions

1. Mix the honey, cinnamon, allspice, nutmeg, and orange zest together in a medium mixing bowl and stir with a wooden spoon until well blended.

2. Add the almonds, apricots, and dates, and continue to stir.

3. Roll into balls, then roll in superfine sugar and serve. Store in an airtight container.

Yield: About 40 sugarplums

Simple Pecan Roll-Ups

This flavorful candy features a luscious cream center covered in caramel and chopped pecans. Unsliced logs wrapped in colored plastic and tied with a pretty ribbon make great gifts.

Ingredients

7 ounces (198 g) marshmallow creme
2¼ cups (270 g) confectioners' sugar
1 teaspoon vanilla extract
¼ cup (½ stick or 60 g) unsalted butter
14 ounces (396 g) caramels
2 tablespoons whipping cream
2 cups (220 g) chopped pecans

Equipment

Medium mixing bowl
Plastic wrap
Double-boiler setup

Instructions

1. Cream marshmallow creme, sugar, vanilla extract, and butter together in a medium mixing bowl. Use your hands to knead mixture until a doughlike consistency is achieved and the sugar is blended thoroughly.

2. Quarter dough and roll into four balls. Shape balls into logs. Wrap each log separately in plastic wrap and put in the freezer to set up.

3. Melt caramels over simmering heat in a double boiler. Add whipping cream and stir until completely blended.

4. Dip candy logs into hot caramel mixture, and immediately roll in chopped pecans. Store logs in refrigerator (wrapped in plastic), and slice just before serving.

Yield: About 40 roll-ups

Milton Hershey's Chocolate

When Milton Hershey died at the age of 88 in October of 1945, the chocolate empire carrying his name had become an American tradition. A man from central Pennsylvania with little education had made one of America's great fortunes.

Though his dogged devotion to the art of making chocolate eventually made him a very wealthy man, Hershey experienced many failures along the way. At age 14, young Milton's father apprenticed him to a printer. When it became apparent that his talents did not lie in printing, Hershey went to work for a candymaker in Lancaster, Pennsylvania. In 1876, at the age of 18, he opened his own candy shop in Philadelphia. The business failed after six years.

Not discouraged, Hershey moved to Denver, Colorado, where he went to work for a caramel manufacturer. From Colorado, Hershey moved on to Chicago, New Orleans, and New York City, trying to establish himself as a candymaker. Finally, he made it back to Lancaster, Pennsylvania, where he began the Lancaster Caramel Company.

Hershey's interest in chocolate took a turn in 1893, when he saw German chocolate-making machinery at the Chicago International Exposition. He purchased his own equipment and began to coat his caramels with chocolate. Believing that a large market existed for affordable chocolate candy that could be mass produced (at that time, milk chocolate was considered a luxury item and was sold in specialty stores), Hershey sold his caramel company in 1900 for $1 million, retaining his equipment and the right to manufacture chocolate.

Hershey moved back to his birthplace, Derry Church, Pennsylvania, and in 1903, began building what is now the world's largest chocolate manufacturing plant. The company thrived under Hershey's guidance, and the community of Hershey (eventually, it became its own town) was built around the operation.

Thus, Hershey had the business acumen to develop the right industry at the right time and, consequently, he made a tremendous fortune. Because Milton Hershey dared to dream of chocolate, today his name conjures delicious associations worldwide.

Historical information is courtesy of Hershey Foods Corporation.

Orange-Butterscotch Balls

These candy balls feature the delectable combination of orange and butterscotch. They freeze wonderfully and last frozen for up to six months.

Ingredients

1 cup (200 g) butterscotch chips
3 tablespoons light corn syrup
½ cup (100 g) granulated sugar
⅓ cup (120 g) frozen orange juice concentrate
2⅔ cups (300 g) crushed vanilla wafers
¾ cup (98 g) chopped cashews
⅛ cup (25 g) superfine sugar

Equipment

Cookie sheet
Wax paper
Double-boiler setup
Rubber spatula
Large mixing bowl
Wooden spoon

Instructions

1. Line a cookie sheet with wax paper and set aside.

2. Melt butterscotch chips in a double boiler over simmering water, stirring frequently with a rubber spatula.

3. When butterscotch is completely melted, add corn syrup, sugar, and orange juice, and continue stirring over low heat until well blended.

4. In a large mixing bowl, combine the wafers, cashews, and the orange-butterscotch mixture. (The wafers are easily crushed with a hammer or a rolling pin in a plastic bag.) Use a wooden spoon to mix the ingredients together thoroughly.

5. Shape the dough into 1-inch (2.5-cm) balls, roll the balls in superfine sugar, and place on the already prepared cookie sheet. Allow to dry for two to three hours. Store in an airtight container.

Yield: About 50 balls

Chewy Apricot Macaroons

If you love macaroons, you won't be able to resist
nibbling on this delicious variation, which includes
dried apricots. These candies are chewy, tangy,
and luscious.

Ingredients

¼ cup (60 g) unsalted butter
1 cup (340 g) light corn syrup
1 cup (200 g) granulated sugar
1 teaspoon salt
1 cup (170 g) finely chopped dried apricots
15 ounces (425 g) sweetened grated coconut

Equipment

Baking pan, 7 x 10 ½ inches (18 x 26.5 cm)
Heavy medium saucepan
Wooden spoon
Candy thermometer
Rubber spatula
Plastic wrap

Instructions

1. Butter the baking pan and set aside.

2. Combine the butter, corn syrup, sugar, and salt in a medium saucepan over high heat. Stir the mixture constantly with a wooden spoon until it comes to a boil.

3. Clip a candy thermometer to the side of the saucepan, reduce to medium heat, and continue to cook mixture until the temperature reaches 242° F (117° C).

4. Remove from heat and stir in apricots and coconut. Stir with a wooden spoon until well mixed.

5. Transfer mixture from the saucepan to the prepared baking pan with a spatula. Place in refrigerator until firm to the touch. Cut into 1-inch (2.5-cm) squares and wrap individually in plastic wrap. Serve cold or at room temperature; they hold their shape better when cold.

Yield: About 70 pieces

Mrs. Mulvaney's Penuche Pecans

Penuche is a traditional, brown-sugar-based, fudge-like candy. This recipe combines a basic penuche with crunchy pecan halves to create yummy clusters.

Ingredients

1 cup (145 g) brown sugar
½ cup (100 g) granulated sugar
½ cup (120 g) sour cream
1 teaspoon vanilla
2 cups (220 g) pecan halves

Equipment

Medium saucepan
Candy thermometer
Large mixing bowl
Wax paper

Instructions

1. Combine brown sugar, granulated sugar, and sour cream in a medium saucepan and cook over low heat until 238° F (114° C) is achieved.

2. Place mixture in a large mixing bowl, add vanilla, and beat until mixture begins to thicken.

3. Add pecans and stir until pecans are well coated.

4. Turn pecans out onto wax paper, separate pecans into clusters, and allow to cool. Store at room temperature in an airtight container.

Yield: About 60 clusters

The History of Sugar

It would be difficult to find anyone among us who doesn't love sweet things. We call each other "sweetie," "sugar," and "honey"; we prepare cakes, cookies, and candy for important occasions; we comfort ourselves and others with sweets. Although sugar is now accessible to everyone for very little money, it was once the food of gods—a sweetener that only royalty and the very rich could afford.

This valuable sweetener, which can be extracted from a variety of plants, such as beets and corn, is most commonly made from sugarcane, a plant that grows best in subtropical areas. The word sugar comes from a Sanskrit word *sarkara*, meaning sand or grain. Sometime between 325 BC and AD 325, either the Indians or Persians (it is still disputed which) developed a technique for transforming sugarcane juice into a semicrystalline form.

This early sugar was filled with impurities and had a great deal of molasses (similar to what we think of as brown sugar); a reliable and efficient technique for purifying sugar had not yet been invented. In fact, until the mid-19th century, most of the sugar consumed had a brownish color.

It is believed that the Moors brought sugar to Europe when they arrived in Spain sometime in the 8th century. Until this time, Europeans had only used sugar for medicinal purposes and as a spice. The Moors also brought with them information on making sugar, and a sugar operation was set up in the Atlantic islands, an area well suited for growing sugarcane.

Soon other parts of the world became interested in sugar. It was produced in great quantities in the Mediterranean between AD 700 and 1600. Venice was a leading producer in the 1500s. Sugar was brought to America on Columbus's second voyage, and today the United States is one of the world's largest consumers of processed sugar.

Tangerine Peels Dipped in Dark Chocolate

The slightly bitter flavor of candied tangerine rinds is delicious when dipped in dark chocolate. Although this is not the type of candy you will gobble down by the handful, the distinctive flavor is marvelous as an accompaniment to a number of foods. Try them tucked into a scoop of vanilla ice cream, or as a complement to liqueur.

Ingredients

2 cups (480 ml) water
2 cups (400 g) granulated sugar
¼ cup (85 g) light corn syrup
3 to 4 organically grown tangerines
6 ounces (170 g) bittersweet chocolate, chopped

Equipment

Cookie sheet
Wax paper
Medium saucepan
Cooling rack
Double-boiler setup
Rubber spatula

Instructions

1. Line a cookie sheet with wax paper and set aside.

2. Wash tangerines, then peel and cut the rind into strips of uniform size. (Cut off most of the pulp.)

3. Combine the water, sugar, and corn syrup in a medium saucepan and bring to a boil.

4. Turn off the heat, add tangerine peels to the syrup mixture, and let sit for one hour. After one hour, drain off the syrup.

5. Position the tangerine peels on the cooling rack in one layer. Bake the fruit peels on the rack for five minutes in a 350° F (180° C) oven. After five minutes, reduce the heat to 200° F (90° C) and let the fruit dry out in the oven for four hours. Take fruit peels off the rack and set aside.

6. Melt the chocolate over simmering heat in the double boiler, stirring frequently with a rubber spatula.

7. When the chocolate is the correct temperature for dipping, use your fingers to dip each fruit peel in the chocolate halfway. (You will probably want to shake off the excess chocolate each time you bring a slice out of the chocolate.) Place each dipped peel on the already prepared cookie sheet.

8. After all the slices are dipped, place them in the refrigerator for 15 minutes or until the chocolate has set. Store in an airtight container in the refrigerator for about three weeks or in the freezer for two months.

   Yield: About 36 pieces

Lime Jelly Delights

Lime-flavored jelly squares are a refreshing addition to any summer celebration. They are best when the lime juice is freshly squeezed, though canned lime juice will also work.

Ingredients

½ cup (120 ml) water
2 cups (400 g) granulated sugar
2½ tablespoons gelatin
¼ cup (60 ml) cold water
¾ cup (180 ml) lime juice
Several drops green food coloring
⅛ cup (25 g) superfine sugar

Equipment

Baking pan, 8 x 8 inches (20.5 x 20.5 cm)
Medium saucepan
Candy thermometer
Small mixing bowl
Whisk

Instructions

1. Butter the baking pan and set aside.

2. Combine water and sugar in a medium saucepan and clip thermometer to the side of the pan. Cook over medium heat until the mixture reaches 255° F (123° C).

3. Soak gelatin in the cold water in a small mixing bowl for about five minutes, then add to cooked syrup. Remove from heat, add lime juice and food coloring, and use whisk to blend mixture.

4. Pour mixture into prepared baking pan. Set aside for several hours or until firm.

5. Turn out of pan onto a cutting surface, cut into squares, then roll in superfine sugar.

Yield: About 50 pieces

Pineapple Cream Candy

This candy is one of my favorite spring and summer recipes, and I often suggest it for weddings or bridal showers. Pineapple and cream is a match made in heaven, especially when combined with chopped pecans and a hint of lemon.

Ingredients

1 cup (200 g) granulated sugar
½ cup (70 g) brown sugar
¼ cup (60 ml) whipping cream
½ cup (125 g) pineapple pulp and juice, canned or fresh
1 tablespoon unsalted butter
¾ cup (86 g) chopped pecans
1 teaspoon lemon extract

Equipment

Cookie sheet
Medium saucepan
Candy thermometer
Pastry brush
Medium mixing bowl
Electric rotary beater or wooden spoon

Instructions

1. Butter a cookie sheet and set aside.

2. Combine both sugars, cream, and pineapple in a medium saucepan. Bring to a boil, then cook over medium heat to 240° F (115° C). Wash down the sides of the pan several times with a pastry brush that has been dipped in cold water, to prevent sugar crystallization.

3. Stir in butter, then remove from heat and transfer to a medium mixing bowl. Add nuts and lemon extract, and beat together. (An electric rotary beater works best, but a wooden spoon can also be used.) Continue to beat until mixture becomes smooth and creamy.

4. Drop by the spoonful onto prepared cookie sheet. Store at room temperature in an airtight container.

Yield: About 25 pieces

Clusters, Candy Balls, and Caramels

Irish Cream Clusters

These creamy treats are flavored with Irish cream liqueur and have only the faintest hint of chocolate. A perfect ending to a festive dinner party.

Ingredients

½ cup (120 ml) whipping cream
1 ounce (28 g) semisweet chocolate, chopped
⅓ cup (80 ml) Irish cream liqueur
2 cups (400 g) granulated sugar
2 tablespoons dark corn syrup
2 tablespoons butter
1½ cups (165 g) chopped pecans

Equipment

Double-boiler setup
Rubber spatula
Candy thermometer
Wax paper

Instructions

1. Combine whipping cream and chocolate in a double boiler over low heat. Stir frequently with a rubber spatula until chocolate is completely melted.

2. Add Irish cream liqueur, sugar, and dark corn syrup. Bring to a boil over medium heat and stir until sugar is dissolved.

3. Clip candy thermometer to the side of the pan and continue to boil over moderately low heat until 234° F (112° C) is achieved.

4. Remove from heat, add butter, and set aside for about five minutes.

5. Beat by hand (with a spoon) until mixture thickens and has a less-glossy finish. Stir in nuts, then quickly spoon mixture onto wax paper.

Yield: About 35 clusters

Dreamy Almond-Cream Caramels

Here's a luscious caramel recipe with added richness
for those occasions in which a little decadence is in
order. Be careful, though; these are addictive.

Instructions

2 cups (480 ml) whipping cream
2 cups (400 g) granulated sugar
1 cup (340 g) light corn syrup
½ cup (1 stick or 115 g) unsalted butter
½ teaspoon salt
½ teaspoon vanilla extract
½ cup (45 g) chopped almonds

Equipment

Baking pan, 8 x 8 inches (20.5 x 20.5 cm)
Small saucepan
Large saucepan
Pastry brush
Candy thermometer

Instructions

1. Butter the baking pan and set aside.

2. In a small saucepan, heat the whipping cream until warm.

3. In a large saucepan, combine half of the heated cream with the sugar and the corn syrup. Bring to a boil over medium-high heat. To prevent sugar crystallization, wash down the sides of the pan several times with a pastry brush that has been dipped in cold water.

4. Carefully stir in the rest of the cream (it will bubble up quite a bit, so go slowly), and cook for about five more minutes.

5. Add butter, one tablespoon at a time.

6. Clip candy thermometer to the side of the pan. When mixture reaches 230° F (110° C), lower heat to medium to prevent scorching. When 245° F (118° C) is achieved, remove pan from heat and let stand for 10 minutes.

7. Carefully add salt, vanilla, and almonds, mix well, then pour into prepared baking pan. Let stand at room temperature until firm, then cut into squares.

Yield: About 70 squares

Lemon-Pistachio Bonbons

A delightful lemon center, a rich chocolate coating,
and a nutty outside make these bonbons an instant
crowd-pleaser.

Ingredients

⅓ cup (80 g or 5⅓ tablespoons) unsalted butter,
at room temperature
2 teaspoons whipping cream
Zest of one lemon
3½ cups (420 g) confectioners' sugar, sifted
12 ounces (340 g) semisweet chocolate chips
1 cup (150 g) finely chopped pistachios

Equipment

Cookie sheet
Wax paper
Medium mixing bowl
Electric rotary beater
Double-boiler setup
Rubber spatula
Fork or other dipping tool

Instructions

1. Line a cookie sheet with wax paper and set aside.

2. Combine the butter, whipping cream, and lemon zest in a medium mixing bowl and cream together ingredients with an electric beater.

3. Gradually add in the confectioners' sugar—1 cup at a time—and blend well. Use your hands to knead the last ½ cup (60 g) of sugar into the mixture.

4. Shape dough into balls, place balls on wax paper, and put in refrigerator until firm.

5. Melt chocolate chips over simmering heat in a double boiler, stirring frequently with a rubber spatula.

6. Use a fork or other dipping tool to dip each ball into chocolate, then roll balls in pistachio nuts. (Wiping off the fork in between steps makes this process easier.) Place back on wax paper and chill until chocolate is firm. Store in an airtight container.

Yield: About 36 bonbons

Variations: Use any other citrus zest for the bonbon center or substitute any other type of nut for pistachios for the crust.

Deanne's Chocolate-Raisin Clusters

This is a wonderful last-minute recipe, and you may have these ingredients in your pantry. It came from my aunt, who has fond memories of making and eating these delectable clusters as a child. They are also great with nuts.

Ingredients

12 ounces (340 g) semisweet chocolate chips
14 ounces (1 can or 396 g) sweetened
condensed milk
1 teaspoon vanilla extract
15 ounces (425 g) raisins

Equipment

Cookie sheet
Wax paper
Double-boiler setup
Rubber spatula
Wooden spoon

Instructions

1. Line a cookie sheet with wax paper and set aside.

2. Melt the chocolate chips with milk and vanilla extract in a double boiler over low heat, stirring frequently with a rubber spatula.

3. When the chocolate is melted and the ingredients are completely mixed together, take saucepan off heat. Use a wooden spoon to blend in raisins and mix together thoroughly.

4. Drop by the spoonful onto the lined cookie sheet. Allow clusters to set up for at least one hour. Store in an airtight container.

Yield: About 60 clusters

The Chocolate Story

When Columbus returned from America and laid an assortment of found treasures at the feet of King Ferdinand and Queen Isabella, surely no one present had any reason to suspect that the few brown beans among Columbus's loot would hold any promise. This was the introduction of cocoa beans, the source of chocolate, to Europe.

Though Columbus brought the first cocoa beans, it was Hernando Cortez, the great Spanish explorer, who was instrumental in making chocolate an important product in Europe. During his conquest of Mexico in the 1500s, Cortez discovered the Aztec Indians were great fans of the cocoa bean. They made a rather bitter drink out of these treasured beans, a drink which they called "chocolatl," meaning warm liquid. Emperor Montezuma was said to consume at least 50 portions of chocolatl every day. Cortez and his countrymen found this chocolatl very bitter and devised the idea of sweetening it with sugar.

Eventually, back in Spain, more ingredients were added, such as cinnamon and other spices, and it was decided the drink tasted better when heated. Spain began to plant cocoa beans in its colonies and kept the secret of how their hot chocolate was made for nearly a hundred years. But the Spanish monks could not keep the secret, and they leaked the story of chocolate; it spread all over Europe—to France, Great Britain, and beyond. Chocolate houses sprang up, and chocolate began to be mass produced.

In the 19th Century, a British company conceived the idea of a solid form of chocolate, which they called *eating chocolate*. In 1876, in Vevey, Switzerland, Daniel Peter came up with the idea of adding milk to chocolate, creating *milk chocolate*. The first chocolate factory was established in America in 1765, and the production of chocolate gained an important position very quickly.

Easy Strawberry-Chocolate Balls

Chocolate and fruit are a wonderful combination; any fruit preserves can be substituted for strawberry preserves here. Make sure you use high-quality preserves, though, as they constitute the predominant flavor.

Ingredients

8 ounces (226 g) cream cheese
6 ounces (170 g) semisweet chocolate chips
1 cup (113 g) vanilla wafers, crushed
¼ cup (72 g) strawberry preserves
1 cup (85 g) chopped, toasted almonds

Equipment

Medium mixing bowl
Electric rotary beater
Double-boiler setup
Rubber spatula
Wooden spoon

Instructions

1. Beat cream cheese in a medium mixing bowl with an electric beater until fluffy.

2. Melt chocolate morsels over low heat in a double boiler, stirring frequently with a rubber spatula.

3. Add melted chocolate to the cream cheese and continue to beat until smooth. Stir in wafer crumbs and strawberry preserves, and blend together with a wooden spoon.

4. Cover mixing bowl and put in refrigerator for about one hour to chill.

5. Form strawberry mixture into balls, then roll in almonds. Store in an airtight container in the refrigerator.

Yield: About 45 balls

Quick Carob Crunches

Though not as sweet as chocolate, carob has an unusual, malty flavor and is caffeine-free. If prepared in the microwave, these crunches take about five minutes to make. If carob is not your thing, use the same amount of milk chocolate morsels.

Ingredients

1½ cups (258 g) carob chips
½ cup (120 g) dried cranberries
1½ cups (42 g) crispy rice cereal

Equipment

Cookie sheet
Double-boiler setup or microwave oven
Rubber spatula

Instructions

1. Grease a cookie sheet and set aside.

2. Melt the carob chips, either in a double boiler over low heat or in the microwave. (It should take about two minutes in the microwave.)

3. When the carob is completely melted, take off heat or remove from microwave and mix in the cranberries and rice cereal with a rubber spatula until thoroughly blended.

4. Drop by the spoonful onto the already prepared cookie sheet, and refrigerate until candy is solid, approximately one hour.

Yield: About 25 crunches

The Gift of Candy

Although candy is often regarded as an elegant festive-occasion food, it is also highly valued as the ultimate "comfort food." For this reason, it makes a wonderful gift; don't forget a holiday hostess, an unsuspecting neighbor, or that overstressed friend. And some candies, including gumdrops, lollipops, and jelly beans, do not contain fat or cholesterol and are low in calories, so you need not worry about jeopardizing the health of the recipient.

Like any other gift, however, presentation is half the battle. Always present your candy gifts in an attractive manner that allows for the most intense anticipation on the part of the recipient. Like any other present, enclose your goodies so that the recipient will have to unwrap or otherwise uncover the contents.

It is not necessary to give huge amounts of candy, since candy should be savored in small portions. It is best to individually wrap candy pieces for gift giving, which makes the candy last longer and look more attractive. The candy tin is a reliable container and is available in a wide variety of styles and sizes. (Always assume the recipient will keep the container—that's part of the present.) Lidded baskets, pretty antique bowls, and decorative boxes also work well as containers. Colorful candies are particularly appealing when enclosed in clear containers, such as glass canisters. Embellish the container with ribbon, flowers, and even a tempting piece of candy.

Homemade candy gifts are guaranteed to keep you highly regarded among friends and family!

Lemon Caramels

A subtle hint of lemon gives these caramels a delightful, yet distinctive flavor. They are sinfully delicious when dipped in dark chocolate.

Ingredients

½ cup (120 ml) water
1½ tablespoons lemon extract
2¼ cups (450 g) granulated sugar
1½ cups (360 ml) whipping cream
⅓ cup (113 g) dark corn syrup
2 tablespoons unsalted butter
Vegetable oil

Equipment

Baking pan, 8 x 8 inch (20.5 x 20.5 cm)
Small saucepan
Large saucepan
Pastry brush
Candy thermometer
Heavy knife
Cutting board

Instructions

1. Grease the baking pan thoroughly, using a paper towel to coat all of the surfaces. (A nonstick pan makes releasing the caramel much easier.) Set the pan aside.

2. In a small, heavy-bottomed saucepan, combine the water, lemon extract, and ¾ cup (150 g) of the sugar. Bring the mixture to a boil over medium-high heat, then remove from heat, cover, and let stand until it is time to add it to the caramel—about 10 minutes.

3. In a large saucepan, bring the whipping cream to a boil over medium heat. Add the remaining sugar (1½ cups or 300 g) and the dark corn syrup, and return to a boil. At this point, you will need to wash down the sides of the pan with a pastry brush that has been dipped in warm water several times, to prevent sugar crystallization.

4. Clip a candy thermometer on the side of the pan and increase the heat to medium-high. Continue to cook the mixture, stirring frequently, until it registers 240° F (115° C)—approximately 10 minutes.

5. Stir in the lemon syrup mixture and continue to cook over medium-high heat until the temperature reaches 257° F (125° C). Remove the pan from the heat and quickly stir in the butter.

6. Pour the caramel mixture into the greased pan. Let the caramel cool at room temperature for about three hours.

7. When the caramel has cooled, coat a heavy knife and a cutting board with vegetable oil. Using a table knife, loosen the caramel from the sides of the pan. Turn the caramel over onto the cutting board and release from pan. Cut the caramel into 1-inch (2.5-cm) pieces. Store in an airtight container between sheets of wax paper or plastic wrap.

Yield: About 60 pieces

Mocha Balls

These scrumptious candies are an elegant accompaniment to steaming espresso at a holiday gathering. They are best when made several days ahead and left to marinate.

Ingredients

2½ cups (283 g) chocolate wafer crumbs
3 tablespoons light corn syrup
2 tablespoons cocoa
1 cup (120 g) confectioners' sugar
1 cup (110 g) chopped pecans
½ cup (120 ml) coffee liqueur
Additional confectioners' sugar

Equipment

Large mixing bowl
Food processor (optional)
Electric rotary beater (optional)

Instructions

1. In a large mixing bowl, combine the wafer crumbs, corn syrup, cocoa, and sugar. Mix together thoroughly with a beater or in a food processor. (You may use any plain chocolate cookies for this recipe. Either chop them in a food processor, or crumble them by hand or with a rolling pin in a plastic bag.)

2. Blend in the pecans and the liqueur and mix together to form a stiff dough. Add coffee liqueur as needed to achieve desired consistency. Be careful not to add too much liqueur, as the balls will become sticky.

3. Separate small portions of the dough and shape into bite-size balls. Roll balls in confectioners' sugar. Store in an airtight container. Dust balls with confectioners' sugar before serving.

Yield: About 36 balls

Variations: Substitute vanilla wafers for chocolate wafers, rum or bourbon for the coffee liqueur, or almonds or walnuts for the pecans.

Chocoholism

You probably know some-
one who is a chocoholic.
And what a delicious
affliction it is! Chocolate
has a wonderfully unique,
creamy flavor, a delightful aroma, and, at its best, melts in your
mouth; and it is great combined with a variety of other delectable foods—fruit, dairy products, liqueur, vanilla, coffee, nuts,
and, of course, more chocolate.

In fact, chocolate is among the least expensive addictions one
can have, and its widespread availability allows for instant
gratification. Chocoholics worldwide can find chocolate in a
variety of forms in even the most remote locales. But, like any
other addiction, a true sufferer cannot get enough, and
another fix is always necessary. Chocoholism is at its most
dangerous when combined with another condition—chocolate
snobbery. Indeed, many a chocolate snob has suffered inde-
scribably for lack of suitable chocolate.

There is actually some scientific basis for chocolate craving.
According to one theory, chocolate helps boost
serotonin, a chemical in the brain that
makes people feel relaxed. When
serotonin levels are low, a mes-
sage is sent to the body to eat
foods high in carbohydrates,
such as chocolate. The same
relationship is thought to
exist between endorphins, or
"feel-good" neurotransmit-
ters, and fat consumption.
Thus, chocolate cravings may
also be motivated by the body's
need for fat-containing foods.

Truffles, Fudge, and Chocolates

Mint Chocolate Squares

Although this recipe requires two double boilers (and, if you're lucky, a friend to help stir the chocolate), it is actually quite simple—and certainly worth the extra effort.

Ingredients

1 pound (454 g) dark chocolate, chopped
8 ounces (226 g or about 1¼ cups)
white chocolate chips
5 tablespoons unsalted butter
14 ounces (396 g) sweetened condensed milk
1½ teaspoons vanilla extract
2 teaspoons peppermint flavoring
3 to 6 drops green food coloring

Equipment

Baking pan, 8 x 8 inches (20.5 x 20.5 cm)
Plastic wrap
Two double-boiler setups
Rubber spatula

Instructions

1. Line baking pan with plastic wrap and set aside.

2. Place the two types of chocolate in separate double-boiler setups over medium heat.

3. Add 4 tablespoons of the butter to the dark chocolate and 1 tablespoon of the butter to the white chocolate. Stir both pans frequently until they are both melted and the chocolate and butter are well mixed.

4. Set the pan of dark chocolate off the boiling water and stir in about a cup of the condensed milk (which will be most of it) and the vanilla. Continue to stir until the mixture is thoroughly blended.

5. Pour half of this mixture into the prepared baking pan and replace the rest of the dark chocolate mixture over the hot water on low heat.

6. Set the pan of white chocolate off the boiling water and stir in the rest of the condensed milk, the peppermint flavoring, and the green food coloring. Stir with a rubber spatula until the mixture is completely blended.

7. Gently pour the white-chocolate mixture over the layer of dark chocolate and spread with the spatula. Place in the refrigerator for six to eight minutes.

8. Spread the remaining dark chocolate over the white chocolate layer and place back in the refrigerator. Chill until firm, lift the chocolate from the pan with the plastic, then cut into small squares. Store in an airtight container and keep refrigerated.

Yield: About 70 pieces

Cherry-Chocolate Truffles

These milk chocolate truffles, at once scrumptious and elegant, explode with the tangy flavor of dried cherries. Serve them with liqueur.

Ingredients

1½ pounds (680 g) milk chocolate, chopped
1 cup (240 ml) whipping cream
½ cup (60 g) finely chopped dried cherries
1½ teaspoons almond extract
Cocoa powder for dusting wax paper
2 cups (200 g) chopped walnuts

Equipment

Double-boiler setup
Candy thermometer
Rubber spatula
Small saucepan
Electric beater
Large mixing bowl

Instructions

1. Put chocolate in a double boiler and clip candy thermometer to the pan. Melt chocolate over medium heat, stirring often with a rubber spatula, until the thermometer registers 110° F (43° C).

2. In a small saucepan, scald the cream over medium heat.

3. Take the top pan off the double boiler, and wipe the water off the bottom of the pot. Pour the cream into the chocolate mixture and mix with an electric beater until smooth.

4. Blend in the dried cherries and almond extract. Clean sides and bottom of bowl with rubber spatula as you beat.

5. When the mixture is smooth, pour the truffle mixture into a mixing bowl, cover, and cool in the refrigerator.

6. When the dough is firm, form into balls with your hands and place balls on a piece of waxed paper that has been dusted with cocoa powder.

7. Once all the balls are shaped, roll them in chopped walnuts. Store in refrigerator in an airtight container. These truffles are best when served chilled.

Note: An easy way to get an even coating of walnuts is to rub the palms of your hands with melted chocolate, roll the balls around in the chocolate, then roll them in the nuts.

Yield: About 60 truffles

Amaretto Truffles

Whether you're an amaretto fan, a chocoholic, or just in the mood for something sweet, you'll love these exquisite dark-chocolate truffles. A superb after-dinner treat.

Ingredients

12 ounces (340 g) bittersweet chocolate chips
½ cup (1 stick or 115 g) unsalted butter
2 egg yolks
½ cup (120 ml) whipping cream
¼ cup (60 ml) amaretto liqueur
Cocoa powder

Equipment

Double-boiler setup
Rubber spatula
Medium mixing bowl

Instructions

1. Melt chocolate in a double boiler over hot (not boiling) water, stirring frequently with a rubber spatula.

2. When chocolate is melted, remove from heat and add the butter, one tablespoon at a time.

3. In a medium bowl, beat egg yolks. Gradually add a third of the hot chocolate mixture to the egg yolks and blend thoroughly. Add egg-chocolate mixture to remaining hot mixture (in pan), stirring constantly.

4. Gradually add the whipping cream and amaretto to the mixture.

5. Return to heat and cook for several minutes—until the mixture thickens somewhat and forms a smooth consistency; stir constantly.

6. Cover mixture and place in the refrigerator to set up.

7. When the mixture is firm enough, roll into balls, then roll balls in cocoa powder. Store in an airtight container in the refrigerator. These are best when served chilled.

Yield: About 50 truffles

Peanut Butter Swirl Squares

This fun and simple recipe is great rainy-day entertainment for kids. Peanut butter and chocolate are easily swirled together with a table knife to create candy with a gourmet look.

Ingredients

16 ounces (453 g) white chocolate, chopped
12 ounces (340 g) peanut butter
16 ounces (453 g) milk chocolate chips

Equipment

Baking pan, 10 x 15 inches (25.5 x 38 cm)
Double-boiler setup
Rubber spatula
Microwave-safe bowl
Knife

Instructions

1. Butter baking pan and set aside.

2. Melt white chocolate over simmering heat in a double boiler, stirring frequently with a rubber spatula.

3. Add peanut butter to white chocolate and stir until well blended. Pour peanut butter mixture into prepared pan.

4. Melt milk chocolate chips in the microwave (follow instructions on package) in a microwave-safe bowl.

5. Pour chocolate over peanut butter mixture and swirl with a knife. Put in refrigerator until firm. Cut into squares and store in the refrigerator.

Yield: About 80 pieces

Buckeyes

These divine candies are always a hit among peanut-butter lovers. They can be made a few weeks ahead of time and stored in the freezer.

Ingredients

1 cup (255 g) peanut butter
1½ cups (180 g) confectioners' sugar
½ cup (1 stick or 115 g) unsalted butter,
at room temperature
12 ounces (340 g) semisweet chocolate chips
½ cup (55 g) pecans halves

Equipment

Cookie sheet
Wax paper
Medium mixing bowl
Wooden spoon
Double-boiler setup
Toothpicks or other dipping tool

Instructions

1. Line cookie sheet with wax paper and set aside.

2. Combine peanut butter, confectioners' sugar, and butter in a medium mixing bowl. Blend together with a wooden spoon until thoroughly mixed.

3. Roll mixture into small balls. Let balls chill in the refrigerator.

4. Melt chocolate chips on top of a double boiler over simmering water.

5. Using toothpicks or any other dipping tool, dip peanut butter balls in the chocolate and transfer dipped balls onto wax paper. Position a pecan half on top of each ball and press down slightly. Store in an airtight container in the refrigerator.

Yield: About 45 buckeyes

Storing and Serving Candy

One of the wonderful things about candy is that it can be made days or even weeks ahead of time, as long as it is stored in an airtight container. Most chocolate-based candies should be stored in the refrigerator, also in an airtight container. Chocolate absorbs other odors easily, so take care to separate chocolate candies from other strongly scented foods.

Most other candies (caramels, brittles, mints, and so forth) do best if stored at room temperature. Layer between wax paper and store in an airtight container. Particularly sticky candy, such as caramels and taffy, should be wrapped individually in plastic.

In general, candy should be served at room temperature, though most homemade truffles are best when served chilled; they tend to get too mushy when brought to room temperature. See individual recipes for detailed serving instructions.

Chocolate-Covered Cherries

There's no wonder these candies are among the most popular treats—they're scrumptious! Impress your guests with a platter of homemade chocolate-covered cherries at your next dinner party.

Ingredients

1 box (450 g) confectioners' sugar
½ cup (170 g) light corn syrup
½ cup (1 stick or 115 g) unsalted butter
1 teaspoon vanilla extract
2 jars maraschino cherries, approximately 100 cherries
12 ounces (340 g) semisweet chocolate chips

Equipment

Cookie sheet
Wax paper
Medium mixing bowl
Double-boiler setup
Rubber spatula
Toothpicks, fork, or other dipping tool

Instructions

1. Cover a cookie sheet with wax paper and set aside.

2. In a medium mixing bowl, mix together confectioners' sugar, corn syrup, butter, and vanilla extract. Knead or stir mixture until ingredients are well mixed and smooth.

3. Pinch a small piece of dough off and wrap around each cherry, rolling between hands quickly to prevent sticking and to form a smooth ball. Place on prepared cookie sheet and refrigerate until firm.

4. Melt chocolate chips in a double boiler over simmering heat, stirring frequently with a rubber spatula.

5. Dip cherries in chocolate, using toothpicks, a fork, or any other dipping tool. Place on wax paper and chill until firm. Store in refrigerator in an airtight container. (Do not freeze.)

Yield: About 100 cherries

Mom's Holiday Fudge

Everyone has at least one food that is associated with the holiday season. For me, it's my mother's fudge. She still brings it out when a festive occasion is at hand, and I haven't been able to find a basic fudge recipe that's tastier—or more foolproof.

Ingredients

4½ cups (900 g) granulated sugar
4 tablespoons unsalted butter
⅛ teaspoon salt
14 ounces (396 g) sweetened evaporated milk
2 teaspoons vanilla extract
12 ounces (340 g) semisweet chocolate chips
12 ounces (340 g) German's sweet chocolate, chopped
15 ounces (425 g) marshmallow creme
2 cups (220 g) chopped pecans
Pecan halves, approximately 60

Equipment

Large baking pan
Large saucepan
Large mixing bowl
Rubber spatula
Plastic wrap

Instructions

1. Butter the baking pan and set aside.

2. Combine the sugar, butter, salt, and evaporated milk, and bring to a boil in a large saucepan over medium heat. Allow to boil for six and a half minutes, stirring constantly. Place the vanilla extract, semisweet chocolate, German's chocolate, marshmallow creme, and chopped pecans in a large mixing bowl.

3. Pour the hot mixture over the ingredients in the mixing bowl and beat until all the chocolate is melted.

4. Pour into the already prepared baking pan and gently spread with a rubber spatula. Place pecans halves on fudge in even lines.

5. Allow fudge to sit for three hours, then cut between pecans to form squares. Wrap individually in plastic wrap and store in an airtight container.

Yield: About 60 pieces

Basic Chocolate Truffles

The basic chocolate truffle, for many chocolate lovers, is one of life's simple pleasures. What most people do not realize, though, is how easy they are to make. Let it be your secret.

Ingredients

8 ounces (226 g) milk chocolate chips
⅓ cup (80 ml) whipping cream
⅓ cup (5⅓ tablespoons or 80 g) unsalted butter
Cocoa powder or confectioners' sugar

Equipment

Double-boiler setup
Rubber spatula
Whisk
Cookie sheet
Wax paper

Instructions

1. Melt milk chocolate chips over simmering water in a double boiler, stirring frequently with a rubber spatula.

2. When chocolate is completely melted, add whipping cream and stir together with a whisk.

3. Remove from heat, wipe water from the bottom of the pan, and stir in butter—one tablespoon at a time—until completely melted. Cover and place in the refrigerator for several hours or until firm.

4. Cover a cookie sheet with wax paper. Shape the firm mixture into balls, place balls on wax paper, and return to refrigerator for about an hour or until firm.

5. Roll truffles in cocoa powder or confectioners' sugar and store in an airtight container in the refrigerator. Truffles are best when served chilled.

Yield: About 45 truffles

Molded Peanut Butter Patties

Peanut butter patties are among my favorite molded treats. Don't be afraid to try your hand at molded candies—they are easier than you may think. Candy molds are available in specialty and gourmet shops in a wide variety of styles.

Ingredients

9 ounces (255 g) peanut butter
¼ cup (½ stick or 60 g) unsalted butter,
at room temperature
½ box (9 ounces or 255 g) confectioners' sugar
12 ounces (340 g) milk chocolate chips

Equipment

Medium mixing bowl
Double-boiler setup
Rubber spatula
Candy mold
Plastic paintbrush (optional)

Instructions

1. Cream together the peanut butter, butter, and confectioners' sugar in a medium mixing bowl until a doughlike consistency is achieved.

2. Melt the milk chocolate over simmering water in a double boiler, stirring frequently with a rubber spatula.

3. When the chocolate is completely melted, pour a small amount in each cavity of the mold. (A small, plastic paintbrush works well for painting molds.) Move mold around and tap on hard surface to distribute chocolate evenly and release any air bubbles. Place in refrigerator for five minutes to set.

4. Roll peanut butter mixture into balls, flatten balls slightly, then place in cavities on top of chocolate.

5. Pour melted milk chocolate over the balls, filling the mold cavities completely. Refrigerate for one hour.

    Yield: About 50 pieces, depending on the mold

White Chocolate Truffles

A touch of nutmeg combined with Irish cream liqueur gives these truffles a subtle, but wonderfully unusual flavor. These are elegant as part of a mixed candy tray, especially when served with basic chocolate truffles (see page 90).

Instructions

12 ounces (340 g) white chocolate, chopped
1½ tablespoons Irish cream liqueur
⅓ cup (80 ml) whipping cream
¼ teaspoon grated nutmeg
Cocoa powder

Equipment

Double-boiler setup
Rubber spatula
Whisk
Small bowl
Wax paper

Instructions

1. Melt white chocolate over simmering heat in a double boiler, stirring often with a rubber spatula.

2. When chocolate is completely melted, use a whisk to blend in the liqueur, whipping cream, and nutmeg.

3. Transfer to a small bowl and place in the refrigerator for several hours.

4. When the white chocolate mixture is firm, but still soft, shape into balls by hand and place balls on wax paper.

5. Roll balls in cocoa powder. Truffles can be refrigerated for several days or frozen for several weeks. Best when served chilled.

Yield: About 30 truffles

Oatmeal Fudge

Oatmeal and chocolate have been combined to make delicious confections for ages. This fudge is a modern (and mouth-watering) take on an old-fashioned candy.

Ingredients

½ cup (1 stick or 115 g) unsalted butter
2 cups (400 g) granulated sugar
¼ cup (84 g) cocoa powder
½ cup (118 ml) milk
½ cup (128 g) peanut butter
2½ cups (203 g) quick oats

Equipment

Baking pan, 8 x 8 inches (20.5 x 20.5 cm)
Medium saucepan
Rubber spatula

Instructions

1. Butter the baking pan thoroughly and set aside.

2. Combine the butter, sugar, cocoa, and milk in a medium saucepan and bring to a boil over medium-high heat. Allow to boil vigorously for about one minute.

3. Turn the heat down to medium and stir in peanut butter. Mix with a rubber spatula until the peanut butter mixture is smooth, add the oats, and stir until oats are thoroughly coated.

4. Pour fudge into the already prepared baking pan and set aside for several hours until it sets up. Cut into squares.

Yield: About 30 squares

More Delicious Candy

Butterscotch Crunch

Candymaking doesn't get much easier than this.
This recipe has commercially made candy as an
ingredient; I use butterscotch pieces, but peppermint
is a nice (and colorful) holiday variation.

Ingredients

1 cup (237 g) semisweet chocolate chips
1 cup (237 g) milk chocolate chips
½ teaspoon vanilla flavoring
½ cup (226 g) finely crushed butterscotch candy

Equipment

Baking sheet
Wax paper
Double-boiler setup
Rubber spatula
Metal spatula

Instructions

1. Line baking sheet with wax paper, butter the wax paper, and set aside.

2. Melt the semisweet chocolate chips and the milk chocolate chips over simmering heat in a double boiler, stirring frequently with a rubber spatula.

3. When the chips are melted, blend in vanilla flavoring. Pour mixture into the already prepared baking sheet and sprinkle butterscotch candy over top of the chocolate. Use a metal spatula to gently press candy into chocolate.

4. Place baking sheet in the refrigerator until almost firm, then cut into pieces. Return to refrigerator and allow to set up completely. Cut into squares or use small cutters for shapes.

Yield: About 35 pieces

Rocky Road Candy

This is the ultimate rocky road candy recipe. Among its virtues are two kinds of nuts and lots of fluffy marshmallows. A great Halloween treat.

Ingredients

12 ounces (340 g) semisweet chocolate chips
½ cup (1 stick or 115 g) unsalted butter
10½ ounces (297 g) miniature marshmallows
½ cup (55 g) coarsely chopped pecans
½ cup (55 g) coarsely chopped peanuts

Equipment

Double-boiler setup
Rubber spatula
Sharp knife

Instructions

1. Melt chocolate chips over simmering heat in a double boiler, stirring frequently with a rubber spatula.

2. Add butter—one tablespoon at a time—to melted chocolate and continue to stir. Once mixture is melted and completely blended, set aside and allow to cool to lukewarm.

3. Stir in marshmallows, pecans, and peanuts.

4. Separate mixture into two equal portions, and roll each portion into a log about 2 inches (5 cm) in diameter.

5. Place in refrigerator to chill until firm. Use a sharp knife to slice into ½-inch slices and serve. Store in an airtight container.

Yield: About 50 pieces

Gran's Seafoam

Of all candies, seafoam (and its cousin *divinity*, which is made with granulated sugar only) is the most sensitive to weather. It simply must be made on a clear, cool day to work perfectly. And when it's perfect, nothing beats its delicate flavor. Though it is possible to beat the seafoam by hand, I strongly recommend using an electric beater, as it takes a lot of beating to get seafoam to a smooth and even consistency.

Ingredients

2 cups (290 g) light brown sugar
½ cup (100 g) granulated sugar
½ cup (170 g) light corn syrup
½ cup (120 ml) water
Dash of salt
2 egg whites
1 teaspoon vanilla extract

Equipment

Cookie sheet
Wax paper
Vegetable spray
Small saucepan
Candy thermometer
Medium glass mixing bowl
Electric rotary beater

Instructions

1. Cover a cookie sheet with wax paper, spray the wax paper with vegetable spray, and set aside.

2. Combine the sugars, corn syrup, water, and salt in a small saucepan and bring to a boil over medium heat until the sugar is dissolved. Wash down the sides of the pan with a pastry brush that has been dipped in cold water. Clip candy thermometer to the side of the pan. Cook syrup until it reaches 262° F (129° C), then remove from heat and set aside.

3. Beat the egg whites in a medium mixing bowl. Add the syrup to the eggs, stir in vanilla, and beat until the mixture holds its shape. (Be patient: if you do not beat this candy long enough, it will not set up properly.)

4. Drop by the spoonful onto the cookie sheet. Set aside to cool overnight uncovered.

Yield: About 50 pieces

Coconut-Cashew Puffs

These baked candies literally melt in your mouth.
Beating shredded coconut and egg whites together
creates a light, fluffy texture, and chopped cashews
provide a subtle crunch.

Ingredients

4 egg whites
¼ teaspoon salt
1¼ cups (250 g) granulated sugar
2½ cups (185 g) sweetened grated coconut
¾ cup (98 g) chopped cashews
Zest of ½ orange

Equipment

Cookie sheet
Wax paper
Electric rotary beater
Large mixing bowl
Rubber spatula
Cooling rack
Metal spatula

Instructions

1. Line a cookie sheet with wax paper and set aside.

2. Beat the egg whites and salt with an electric rotary beater in a large mixing bowl until soft peaks form. Add the granulated sugar gradually and continue to beat until mixture is very stiff.

3. Carefully fold in coconut, cashews, and orange zest with a rubber spatula.

4. Drop by the spoonful onto prepared cookie sheet and bake at 325° F (160° C) for 20 minutes or until just brown. Slip wax paper from the cookie sheet onto a damp towel, then transfer drops to a cooling rack with a metal spatula. Store in airtight container.

Yield: About 40 puffs

Irish Potato Candy

The use of potatoes as a base for candy recipes dates back to the pioneer days. This delicious recipe is very easy—and is a great way to make use of left-over cooked potatoes.

Ingredients

3 potatoes, each about the size of an egg
1½ pounds (685 g) confectioners' sugar
12 ounces (340 g) chilled peanut butter

Equipment

Small saucepan (for boiling potatoes)
Mixing bowl
Electric rotary beater or hand masher
Sifter
Wax paper or marble slab
Rubber spatula

Instructions

1. Boil potatoes with jackets on until they are soft. (It is essential that you cook the potatoes thoroughly, or the potato dough will tend to be lumpy.)

2. Peel potatoes and mash in a mixing bowl until smooth, either with an electric rotary beater or a hand masher.

3. Sift sugar and add to the potatoes, ¼ cup (30 g) at a time—this will make a thick dough.

4. Roll out potato dough on a piece of wax paper or a marble slab that has been sprinkled with confectioners' sugar.

5. When the dough is about ¼ inch (.5 cm) thick, use a rubber spatula to spread a layer of chilled peanut butter over the entire surface of the dough. Beginning from one side, carefully roll up the dough/peanut butter mixture into a log. Allow to set for one hour. Slice roll and serve, or store in a covered, airtight container.

Yield: About 60 pieces

Candy Sticks

Marshmallow and caramel blend together to form a rich, creamy center, when sticks of candy are dipped in melted chocolate. A coating of toasted coconut is the perfect finishing touch.

Ingredients

Caramel pieces, about 25 pieces (7 ounces or 198 g)
Miniature marshmallows, about 50 or about
13 regular marshmallows, quartered
14 ounces (396 g) milk chocolate chips
2 cups (152 g) toasted coconut

Equipment

Sucker sticks
Cookie sheet
Wax paper
Double-boiler setup
Rubber spatula

Instructions

1. Push a miniature marshmallow onto the end of a sucker stick, then do the same with a caramel square, then with another marshmallow. Repeat procedure with remaining sucker sticks until caramels and marshmallows are all used. (Each stick should have two marshmallows and one piece of caramel.)

2. Line a cookie sheet with wax paper.

3. Melt milk chocolate over simmering heat in a double boiler, stirring with a rubber spatula.

4. Dip candy (by the sucker stick) into the melted chocolate and immediately roll in toasted coconut. Place candy stick on wax paper, then put in refrigerator for 10 minutes or until set.

Yield: 25 candy sticks

Marzipan Pumpkins

Marzipan is an almond-flavored confection with the consistency of modeling clay; it's fun to make, because it has such a wonderful potential for creative expression. You have probably seen marzipan in a plethora of fruit and vegetable shapes. While we have made miniature pumpkins here, you can add any food color or flavoring and, of course, shape it into anything you like. You can buy marzipan already prepared in the gourmet section of the supermarket, but I would highly suggest that you make your own—it will taste better and cost much less.

Ingredients

1 cup (85 g) blanched almonds
½ cup (100 g) granulated sugar
1½ tablespoons water
½ teaspoon almond extract
1 tablespoon lemon juice
Food coloring (optional)

Equipment

Blender or food processor
Small saucepan
Wooden spoon or spatula
Toothpick, knife, or other sharp tool

Instructions

1. Grind the almonds to a very fine consistency in a blender or food processor. The challenge with marzipan is getting the ingredients to a smooth consistency.

2. Combine the sugar, water, almond extract, and lemon juice in a small saucepan over medium heat; stir constantly with a wooden spoon or spatula until the mixture comes to a boil and forms a syrupy consistency. Boil for 3½ to 4 minutes.

3. Carefully add the syrup to the paste in the food processor and continue to blend until the mixture is well blended. Remove it from the food processor and form it into a ball. Marzipan is best after it has had three to four days to sit.

4. Flavorings for marzipan are endless; some favorites are vanilla, rum, cherry extract, almond extract, lemon juice, or orange-flavored liqueur. For a slightly different, but still delicious marzipan variation, add coconut or marshmallows. Add in flavoring just before you color your paste.

5. To form pumpkins, add a few drops of orange food coloring to a ball of marzipan paste and blend in color thoroughly. Add additional food coloring until the desired color is achieved. Separate the paste into portions that are the size you want the pumpkins to be. Roll the portions into balls, then press the balls down slightly with the palm of your hand. Use a toothpick, knife, or other sharp tool to form lines longitudinally on the pumpkin. Either add a green or brown marzipan stem at the top of each pumpkin or use a clove. For shading, you can also use a small watercolor brush to apply food coloring that has been diluted with water.

Yield: About 12 ounces (340 g) of marzipan paste

Pull Taffy

Your grandmother made it. Chances are, her grandmother made it. Don't you think it's time you tried
your hand at pulling taffy?

Ingredients

2½ cups (500 g) granulated sugar
2 tablespoons cornstarch
2 teaspoons liquid glycerin
1 cup (240 ml) water
1 cup (340 g) light corn syrup
1½ teaspoons salt
3 tablespoons unsalted butter
1 teaspoon vanilla extract
Food coloring (optional)

Equipment

Large baking pan or marble slab
Heavy saucepan
Wooden spoon
Candy thermometer
Culinary scissors or heavy knife
Plastic wrap

Instructions

1. Butter baking pan or marble slab thoroughly.

2. In a lightly oiled, heavy saucepan, combine the sugar and cornstarch, then stir in the glycerin, water, corn syrup, and salt. Heat on medium until the sugar is dissolved, stirring with a wooden spoon.

3. When the mixture comes to a boil, cover and allow to boil for four minutes. Clip candy thermometer to the side of the pan and heat to 270° F (132° C). (Be patient; this may take more than 30 minutes.) Remove mixture from heat and stir in the butter, vanilla extract, and food coloring (if desired).

4. Without scraping the saucepan, pour into prepared baking pan or onto the marble slab. As taffy cools, pull the edges into the center of the candy to keep the edges soft and to help the taffy cool evenly. This makes pulling easier.

5. When the taffy has cooled to lukewarm and is comfortable to handle, butter fingers well and begin pulling taffy. First, form the taffy into a ball, then begin stretching and pulling it into ropelike pieces. The taffy will become lighter in color and texture and more elastic. The more you pull, the more air the taffy will have and the lighter it will be.

6. Form ¾-inch (2-cm) ropes with the taffy, then cut into pieces with buttered scissors or a heavy, buttered knife. Wrap taffy pieces individually in plastic wrap.

Yield: About 100 taffy pieces

Variations: Substitute any other flavoring for vanilla (peppermint oil, orange extract, almond extract, and so forth), or add cocoa or nuts.

Popcorn Balls

Shaping popcorn into balls by hand is a surprisingly satisfying process; also try spreading the sticky popcorn on a cookie sheet and separating it into clusters. Add a few drops of food coloring to make brightly colored candy.

Ingredients

5 quarts (4.8 l) popped popcorn
(1 quart [.9 l] equals 2 cups)

1 cup (200 g) granulated sugar
1 cup (145 g) brown sugar
¼ cup (85 g) dark corn syrup
½ cup (170 g) light corn syrup
4 tablespoons butter
1 cup (240 ml) water
1 teaspoon white vinegar
1 teaspoon vanilla extract
Butter for your hands, about ¼ cup (½ stick or 60 g)

Equipment

Oven-proof container
Large, lidded saucepan
Candy thermometer
Plastic wrap

Instructions

1. Pop the popcorn ahead of time, place in an oven-proof container, and keep in a warm oven.

2. Combine sugars, corn syrups, butter, water, and vinegar in a large saucepan and cook, covered, over medium-high heat until sugar dissolves, or about five minutes.

3. Uncover, clip a candy thermometer to the side of the pan, and cook to 250° F (120° C). Set pan off heat and add the vanilla.

4. Remove the popcorn from the oven and gradually pour mixture over top of it. Stir just until the popcorn is well coated.

5. When popcorn is comfortable to touch, generously coat your hands in butter or cooking spray and shape popcorn into balls. (Make sure the popcorn is cool enough to handle before you begin!) Wrap popcorn balls in plastic wrap and store at room temperature.

Yield: 15 to 20 balls

Cream Cheese Mints

One taste of these rich and creamy treats, and you'll
wonder why you ever bothered with
store-bought mints.

Ingredients

3 ounces (85 g) cream cheese, at
room temperature
3 cups (360 g) confectioners' sugar
5 to 6 drops mint flavoring
5 to 6 drops food coloring (optional)
½ cup (100 g) superfine sugar

Equipment

Cookie sheet
Wax paper
Large mixing bowl
Electric beater
Cutting board
Mold or small cutters (optional)

Instructions

1. Line the cookie sheet with wax paper and set aside.

2. In a large mixing bowl, beat the cream cheese until soft. Gradually beat in 2½ cups (300 g) of the confectioners' sugar.

3. Dust a cutting board with the remaining confectioners' sugar (½ cup or 60 g), remove the mixture from the bowl, and knead on the cutting board until a doughy consistency is achieved. Add sugar as needed to adjust consistency.

4. Add the flavoring, then the food coloring, if desired.

5. Pinch off small sections and form into balls. Roll the balls in the superfine sugar. Either serve as mint balls, flatten the balls into patties, press the dough into molds, or use small cutters to form into shapes. Place mints on the cookie sheet and put aside to set up for at least two hours. Store in refrigerator in an airtight container.

Yield: About 40 mints

Maple Buttercreams

Buttercream filling can be made weeks ahead of time, wrapped in plastic, and stored in the refrigerator. These delectable buttercreams are fabulous and foolproof; substitute any flavoring of your choice for maple, if you wish.

Ingredients

⅓ cup (5⅓ tablespoons or 80 g) unsalted butter
⅓ cup (113 g) light corn syrup
½ teaspoon vanilla extract
1½ teaspoons maple flavoring (or to taste)
3 cups (360 g) confectioners' sugar
12 ounces (340 g) milk chocolate chips

Equipment

Cookie sheet
Wax paper
Medium mixing bowl
Electric rotary beater or wooden spoon
Double-boiler setup
Toothpicks or dipping spoon

Instructions

1. Line cookie sheet with wax paper and set aside.

2. Combine the butter, corn syrup, vanilla extract, and maple flavoring in a medium mixing bowl. Gradually add the confectioners' sugar while blending with an electric beater or wooden spoon.

3. Roll buttercream filling into balls, place on prepared cookie sheet, and put in the refrigerator for about 30 minutes. Remove from refrigerator and allow buttercreams to come to room temperature.

4. Melt the chocolate in a double boiler over simmering (not boiling) water. Using a toothpick or dipping spoon, dip each buttercream ball into the chocolate, put back on cookie sheet, then place in the refrigerator. Store these in refrigerator in an airtight container.

Yield: About 60 buttercreams

Nanaimo Bars

Nanaimo bars are a favorite treat of a friend of mine, Jennifer Dent. A traditional Canadian dessert, these decadent bars are named after the city with the same name on Vancouver Island.

Ingredients

For the crust:
½ cup (1 stick or 115 g) unsalted butter
¼ cup (50 g) sugar
5 tablespoons cocoa
1 teaspoon vanilla
1 egg
¾ cup (90 g) sweetened grated coconut
1¾ cups (207 g) graham cracker crumbs
½ cup (50 g) chopped walnuts

For the cream:
¼ cup (½ stick or 60 g) unsalted butter
1 cup (106 g) instant vanilla pudding mix
1 cup (240 ml) milk
1 cup (240 ml) water

For the topping:
1 tablespoon unsalted butter
3 ounces (85 g) semisweet chocolate

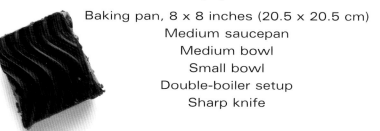

Equipment

Baking pan, 8 x 8 inches (20.5 x 20.5 cm)
Medium saucepan
Medium bowl
Small bowl
Double-boiler setup
Sharp knife

Instructions

1. Grease the baking pan and set aside.

2. In a medium saucepan, combine the butter (½ cup or 115 g), sugar, cocoa, and vanilla over medium heat. Beat in egg and stir constantly until a smooth and slightly thickened consistency is achieved.

3. Remove from heat and stir in the coconut, graham cracker crumbs, and walnuts. Press the mixture into the prepared baking pan.

4. To make the middle layer, cream the butter in a medium bowl.

5. In a small bowl, mix together the vanilla pudding mix, milk, and water.

6. Add vanilla pudding mixture to the creamed butter. Spread the creamy mixture over the crust and chill for about 15 minutes.

7. Melt chocolate with 1 tablespoon butter over medium heat in a double boiler. Spread chocolate over second layer.

8. Let sit for several minutes, then chill in the refrigerator until set (about one hour). Cut into squares with a sharp knife.

Yield: About 36 bars

Confetti Candy

Many candy enthusiasts make nonpareils using this technique, and indeed it's an easy way to make colorful candy quickly. Candy supply stores now have a variety of candy sprinkles for nearly every holiday or occasion: Christmas trees, tiny wreaths, red hearts, and so forth.

Ingredients
8 ounces (226 g) white chocolate
2.8-ounce (79-g) container of confetti sprinkles

Equipment
Double-boiler setup
Rubber spatula
Squeeze bottle
Cookie sheet
Small plastic funnel (optional)

Instructions

1. Melt white chocolate over simmering water in a double boiler, stirring frequently with a rubber spatula.

2. When chocolate is completely melted, transfer to the squeeze bottle. (A small plastic funnel works well for this purpose.) Cut the tip off the squeeze bottle.

3. Spread confetti sprinkles on the cookie sheet in a thin, even layer.

4. Squeeze small circles of white chocolate onto the confetti candy. Make sure the circles do not run together, but do not space them too far apart, as this wastes confetti candy. (You will have excess confetti candy, which can be collected and reused.)

5. Place the cookie sheet in the refrigerator for about 10 minutes or until the candy has set up.

   Yield: About 75 pieces, depending on size

Butterscotch-Cream Cheese Squares

These delightful candy squares are an attractive addition to any autumn party or tailgate lunch. Substitute peanut butter chips for butterscotch for a just-as-delicious variation.

Ingredients

8 ounces (226 g) butterscotch chips
8 ounces (226 g) cream cheese
1¾ cups (210 g) confectioners' sugar
8 ounces (226 g) milk chocolate chips
1 cup (74 g) toasted coconut

Equipment

Baking pan, 8 x 8 inches (20.5 x 20.5 cm)
Double-boiler setup
Rubber spatula
Whisk
Sharp knife

Instructions

1. Butter the baking pan and set aside.

2. Melt the butterscotch in a double boiler over simmering heat, stirring frequently with a rubber spatula.

3. When butterscotch is completely melted, stir in the cream cheese, a small chunk at a time, and blend thoroughly.

4. Remove top of double boiler from heat, wipe off bottom of pan, and add in the confectioners' sugar gradually, stirring with a whisk.

5. Use a rubber spatula to spread mixture into buttered baking pan. Place in the freezer to firm up.

6. Melt chocolate in a double boiler over simmering water, stirring frequently.

7. Pour melted chocolate over firm butterscotch mixture in pan, sprinkle chocolate with toasted coconut, then put in refrigerator until firm. It is easiest to cut candy into squares by turning it out of the pan, coconut facing down, and cutting with a sharp knife. Store in an airtight container in the refrigerator.

Yield: About 75 squares

Troubleshooting

Undercooked Candy

You can mix dry fondant (available at candy supply stores) with some candy to harden it. If melted chocolate is added to candy before it cools, it will make the candy firm when it cools.

Overcooked Candy

If the candy is scorched, there is no way to save it. If it is only slightly overcooked, simply add water or milk (or whatever liquid was used in the recipe) to the still-cooking candy. This will drop the candy's temperature several degrees to the desired temperature.

Recooking Candy

It is possible to recook caramels and fudges, that have been undercooked or overcooked, though the candy will have a darker color. Simply place the candy back over heat and add 1½ cups (360 ml) of water. Stir over low heat until well blended, then bring to boil over medium heat. Clip on the candy thermometer and bring to the correct temperature. Proceed as the original recipe instructs. Since the old flavoring may have cooked away, add more.

Botched Seafoam or Divinity

Divinity is tricky. If it does not set up properly, you cannot recook it. If it is undercooked, simply stir in ¼ cup (30 g) confectioners' sugar with a wooden spoon. If it is overcooked, add a tablespoon of hot water and mix with a wooden spoon. Continue to add water—a tablespoon at a time—until the mixture forms soft peaks.

Candy Boils Over

This is usually caused by inattention. It also happens when milk-based candies are covered with a lid while they cook. Watch candy closely and constantly, adjusting heat as often as necessary. But don't worry, it happens to the best chefs. Pull the pan off the heat, and either clean the burner thoroughly or move candy to another burner.

Candy Does Not Set Up

Candy made in humid, overcast weather may not set up properly. A clear, cool day is the perfect day for candymaking.

WEIGHT EQUIVALENTS

3 teaspoons	= 1 tablespoon
2 tablespoons	= 1 fluid ounce
4 tablespoons	= ¼ cup
8 tablespoons	= ½ cup
16 tablespoons	= 1 cup
1 pint	= 2 cups
2 pints	= 1 quart
1 quart	= 4 cups

Brown Sugar	1 cup	5 ounces	145 g
Butter	4 sticks (2 cups)	1 pound	454 g
Chocolate		1 pound	454 g
Confectioners' sugar	1 cup	4 ounces	120 g
Corn syrup, molasses, maple syrup	1 cup	8 fl. ounces (12 ounces by weight)	340 g
Granulated sugar	1 cup	7 ounces	200 g
Nuts			
Almonds, sliced	1 cup	3 ounces	85 g
Cashews	1 cup	4½ ounces	130 g
Hazelnuts	1 cup	4½ ounces	130 g
Macadamia nuts	1 cup	4 ounces	110 g
Peanuts	1 cup	4 ounces	110 g
Pecans	1 cup	4 ounces	110 g
Pistachio nuts	1 cup	5 ounces	150 g
Walnuts	1 cup	3½ ounces	100 g
Dry measurements	1 cup	16 tablespoons	
Liquid measurements	1 cup (8 fl. ounces)	16 tablespoons	240 ml

TEMPERATURE EQUIVALENTS

200° to 205° F	= 95° C	370° to 375° F	= 190° C
220° to 225° F	= 105° C	400° to 405° F	= 205° C
245° to 250° F	= 120° C	425° to 430° F	= 220° C
275° F	= 135° C	445° to 450° F	= 230° C
300° to 305° F	= 150° C	470° to 475° F	= 245° C
325° to 330° F	= 165° C	500° F	= 260° C
345° to 350° F	= 175° C		